# Theseus and the Minotaur

*Written by C.J. Naden*
*Illustrated by Robert Baxter*

**Troll Associates**

# Pronunciation Guide

| | |
|---|---|
| Aegeus | (EE-jee-us) |
| Ariadne | (ar-ee-AD-nee) |
| Crete | (KREET) |
| Dionysus | (dy-uh-NY-sus) |
| Minos | (MY-nos) |
| Minotaur | (MIN-uh-tor) |
| Sciron | (SY-run) |
| Sinis | (SY-nis) |
| Theseus | (THEE-see-us) |

Copyright © 1981 by Troll Associates
All rights reserved. No part of this book may be used or reproduced
in any manner whatsoever without written permission from the publisher.
Printed in the United States of America. Troll Associates, Mahwah, N.J.
Library of Congress Catalog Card Number: 80-50067
ISBN 0-89375-363-7    (0-89375-367-X soft cover ed.)

L ong, long ago, the city of Athens was a dangerous place. Thieves lurked in dark corners. Bandits and murderers attacked travelers on the roads. The people lived in fear for their lives.

King Aegeus was
especially afraid for
the life of his son, who
was called Theseus. So he
sent the child far away from
Athens to grow up in safety.
When Theseus was a young
man, his mother took him to
a lonely wood. She pointed
to a huge stone and asked,
"Are you strong enough
to move that?"

4

Theseus was anxious to prove his strength, so he pushed and tugged at the stone. But it would not move. "Very well," said his mother, "that is enough." But Theseus wanted to try once more. This time the stone rolled away. Beneath it lay a silver sword with the words "I am the sword of Aegeus" written on it.

"Your father put the sword here many years ago," said his mother. "He said that if you could move the stone, you would be strong enough to fight the enemies of Athens." Theseus was very excited at the thought of joining his father. And to prove how brave he was, he decided to travel by land. Bandits and murderers ruled the roads to Athens, but he would destroy them!

Very soon, Theseus met his first test. Before him in the road stood Sinis, the pine bender. This monster liked to bend down pairs of pine trees and tie his victims to the tops. When the trees sprang up like arrows, they ripped apart the helpless travelers. Sinis thought this was great sport. His laugh could be heard for miles whenever he found a new victim.

But Sinis did not laugh for long when he met Theseus. Before the monster could move, Theseus grabbed him and tied him to the tops of two tall pine trees. "Let me hear you laugh now," Theseus said as he cut the ties. The tall pine trees shot upward, and the cruel monster went to his death.

The next day Theseus came upon another terrible monster. He
was known as Sciron, the kicker. Sciron amused himself by
kicking travelers over a cliff. Waiting below was his giant,
flesh-eating tortoise. "My pet is very hungry," called Sciron
when he saw Theseus standing in the road. "I can see that you
will make a fine meal."

But Sciron was wrong. Theseus rushed at the evil kicker and lifted him high into the air. "We will see which one makes a fine meal," Theseus cried. Then he tossed Sciron over the cliff. The hungry giant tortoise opened its huge jaws and snapped him in two!

By the time Theseus reached Athens, everyone had heard of him. People crowded the streets to wave and cheer. "Who is he?" they asked. "If he can kill Sinis and Sciron, perhaps he can rid us of *all* our enemies." King Aegeus wondered about the young warrior, too. He was anxious to meet such a brave man.

The King called Theseus to the palace. Without speaking, the young man drew out the silver sword. King Aegeus could not believe what he saw. Here was his son, grown now into a strong and brave warrior. Tears of happiness filled the old King's eyes.

The people of Athens were happy, too. Now they had some-
one with great strength and courage to fight their enemies.
Theseus would protect them from anything. And Theseus did
protect the city. In a short time, Athens was peaceful once
again. It was safe now for his mother, the Queen, to join
them.

But happiness did not last long in Athens. By the next spring, Theseus began to notice that the people once again looked sad and afraid. "What is the matter with them?" he asked his father. "The city is peaceful now. There is nothing to fear." The old King shook his head and told Theseus the story of Minos and the Minotaur.

Many years before, King Minos of Crete had sent his only son to Athens. The boy took part in the annual athletic games. But through a sad accident, the boy was killed. King Minos wanted revenge. But, instead of destroying Athens with his powerful army, he demanded a different — and more terrible — payment. Every nine years, seven young men and seven young women must be sent to Crete. There they would be thrown to the Minotaur. Now, once again, the ninth year had come.

15

Theseus understood why the people of Athens were sad and afraid. He said to his father, "This year I will go to Crete as one of the hostages. But I will not die, Father. I am going to kill the Minotaur!" The old King did not believe that anyone could kill the Minotaur, but he was proud of his son's courage.

16

"I will watch each day for your ship's return," said the King. "When it sails into the harbor, do not fly the usual black sails. That will mean that you have died. Fly a white sail instead. Then I will know that you are alive." Theseus promised to do as his father asked. Then he and the other young people sailed for Crete.

When they reached Crete, the hostages were put into cells. In the morning, they would face the Minotaur. The Minotaur was a monster, half-bull, half-human. It was taller than two men and twice as strong. The Minotaur lived in the center of a huge maze of twisting passages. When people entered the maze, they wandered about, and soon were hopelessly lost. They could never find their way out. The Minotaur would find *them*!

That night, Princess Ariadne, the daughter of King Minos, came to see the prisoners. When she saw handsome young Theseus, she fell in love with him at once. "I must save him from the Minotaur," Ariadne said to herself, "even though my father will never forgive me."

Before dawn the next morning, Ariadne said to Theseus,
"Take this golden thread. Tie it to the entrance as you enter
the maze. Unwind the thread as you go. The monster will be
sleeping at this early hour. When you have killed it, follow the
thread back to the entrance. Take this sword with you."

Theseus was surprised that the King's daughter would help
him. "How can I repay you?" he asked. "You must take me
with you when you escape," Ariadne replied. "When my
father learns what I have done, he will kill me." Theseus
promised to do as she asked.

Ariadne led Theseus to the entrance of the maze. He tied the golden thread to the gate. Then he entered the maze, unwinding the thread as he walked. For what seemed like hours, Theseus wandered through the twisting passages. Without the thread, he knew he would be hopelessly lost. In the distance, he could hear the heavy breathing of the sleeping monster.

Suddenly, Theseus came upon a wide clearing. There, before
him on the floor, was the huge, hideous beast. The Minotaur
heard Theseus' footsteps, and jumped quickly to its feet. It began to snarl and roar. For a moment, Theseus could not even
draw his sword. The Minotaur was so tall and so horrible that
Theseus was frozen with fear.

Then the Minotaur charged at Theseus. Theseus drew his
sword. The Minotaur leaped into the air, and Theseus plung-
ed the sword deep into its body. The monster screamed in
agony and fell to the floor. With a lightning stroke, Theseus
cut off its head.

Carefully, Theseus followed the golden thread back to the entrance. There he found Ariadne and the others waiting for him. "Quickly, we must go to your ship!" Ariadne cried. She led them all to the sea, where they set sail immediately.

The Athenians could not believe that they were free. They called Theseus the greatest of all heroes. "But it is Princess Ariadne who saved us," said Theseus. "And before we make the long journey to Athens, we must all rest." So the small party stopped for a day and a night on a deserted island.

A terrible tragedy happened on the island. Some say that Theseus had a dream in which he was warned that Ariadne would betray him. So he set sail without her. When Ariadne awoke, she was heartbroken to find she had been deserted. But Dionysus, the youngest of the great gods, came to her. He placed a crown upon her head and took her into the heavens to be his wife.

Others say that Theseus did not leave Ariadne. Instead, she died on the island that night. Theseus was filled with sadness. After he buried Ariadne, Theseus and the other Athenians boarded the ship and sailed for home.

Perhaps because Theseus was so overcome with grief, he forgot his promise to his father. He did not raise the white sails of his ship. When King Aegeus saw the black sails coming into the harbor, he thought his son had died. The King was so sorrowful that he threw himself into the sea and drowned.

Theseus sailed his ship into the harbor and searched for his father. The Queen came forward and said, "The King is dead." Then she pointed to the black sails. Theseus looked up in horror. He could not believe what he had done. His forgetfulness had caused his father's death.

Theseus never forgot this terrible lesson. But he kept the name of his father sacred. And he tried to be a good King in his place. He ruled Athens with kindness and justice. Peace and happiness came again to the ancient city.

Athenians believed that the gods smiled on Theseus. He was a man of many faults. But he was also a man of strength and bravery and kindness. And while he was King, Athens became known as the glory of all Greece.